POPULAR SONGS

★ FOR EASY CLASSICAL GUITAR ★

ARRANGED BY MARK PHILLIPS

ISBN 978-1-4803-9547-3

HAL•LEONARD®
CORPORATION

7777 W. BLUEMOUND RD. P.O. BOX 13819 MILWAUKEE, WI 53213

T0057665

For all works contained herein:

Beauty and the Beast

from Walt Disney's BEAUTY AND THE BEAST

Lyrics by Howard Ashman
Music by Alan Menken

Moderately slow

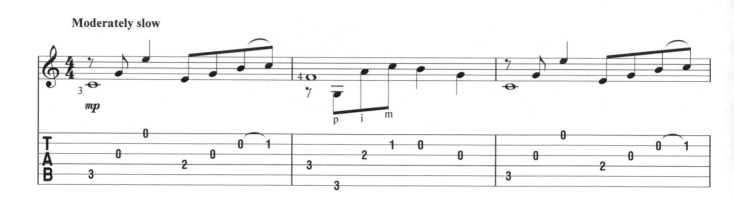

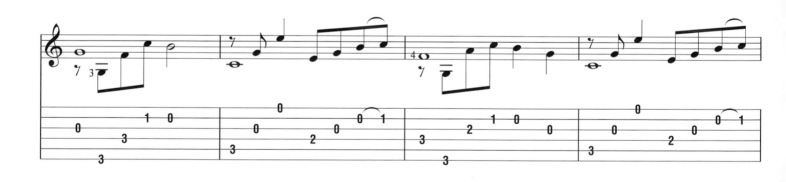

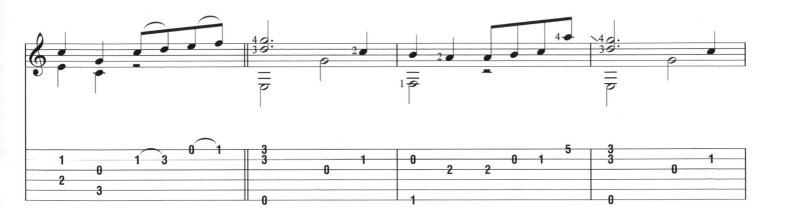

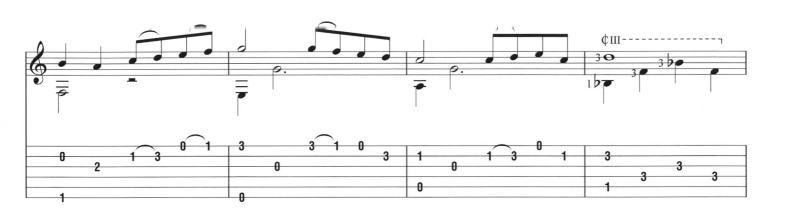

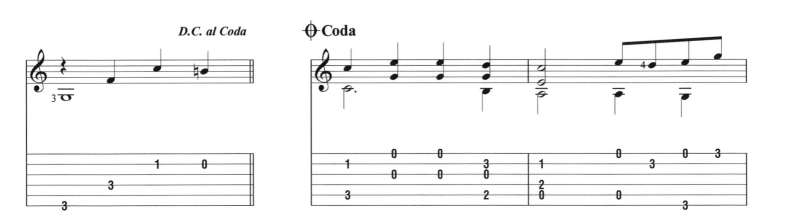

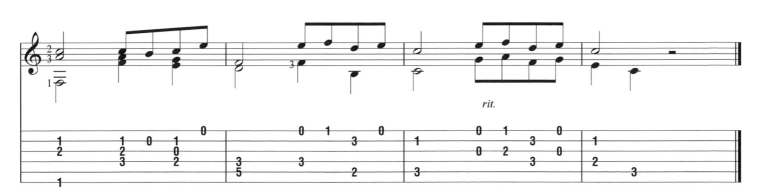

Ben

Words by Don Black
Music by Walter Scharf

Moderately slow

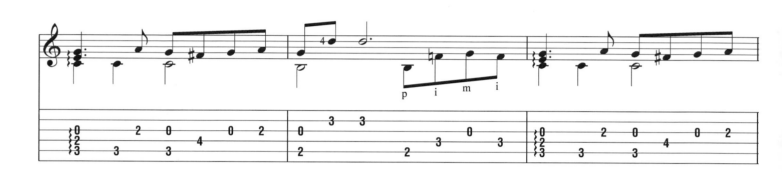

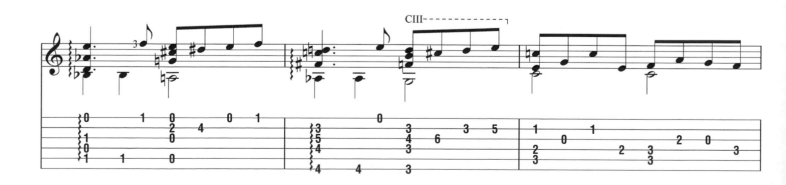

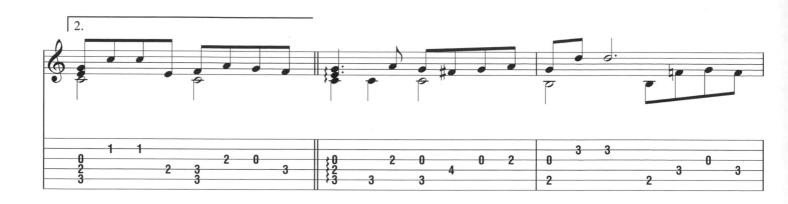

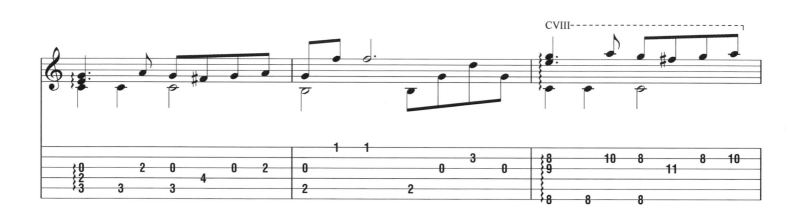

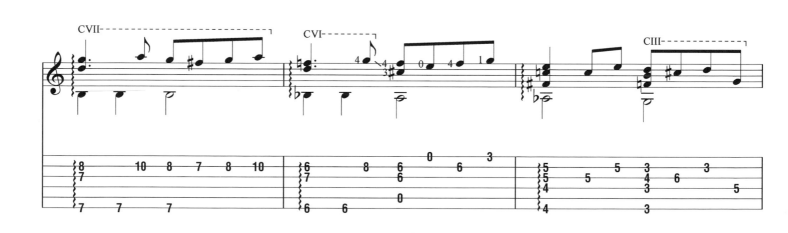

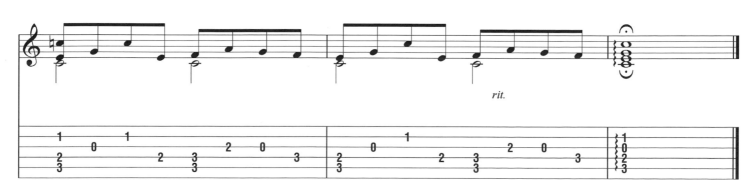

Somewhere Out There

from AN AMERICAN TAIL

Music by Barry Mann and James Horner
Lyric by Cynthia Weil

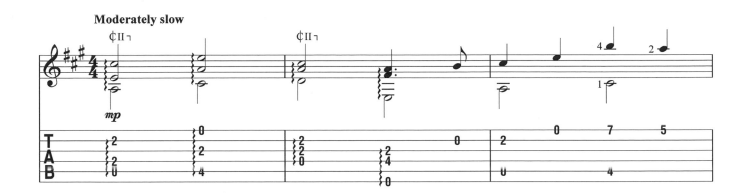

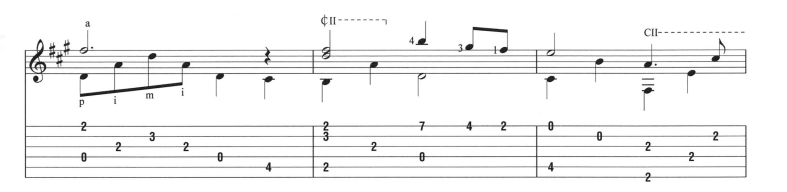

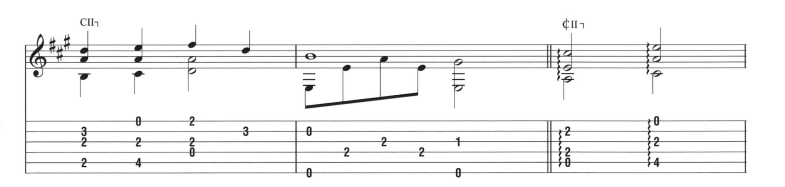

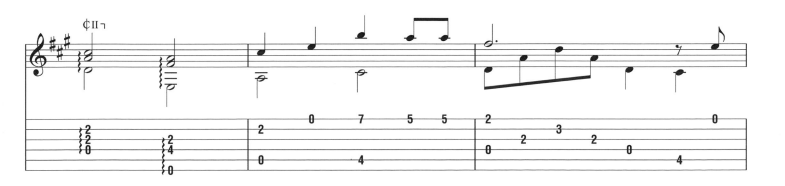

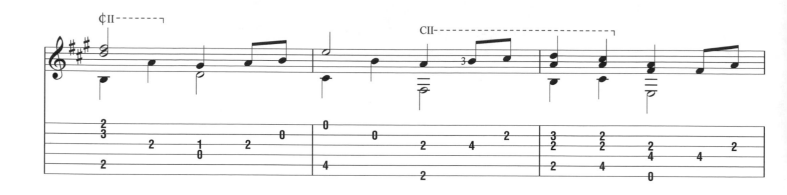

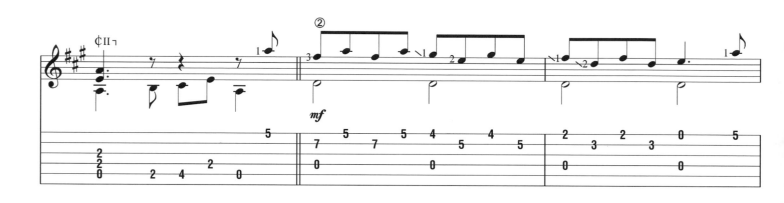

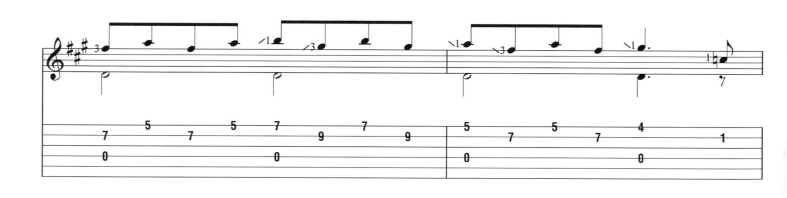

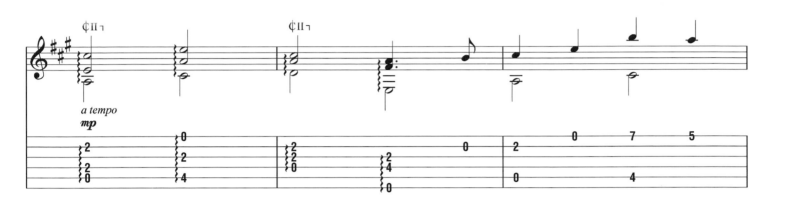

Can You Feel the Love Tonight

from Walt Disney Pictures' THE LION KING

Music by Elton John
Lyrics by Tim Rice

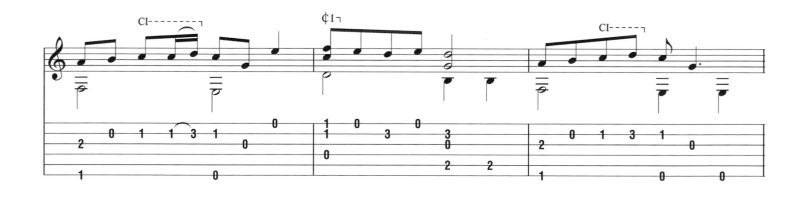

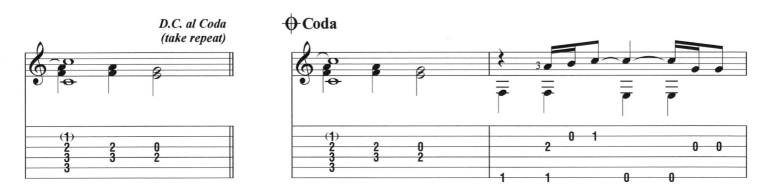

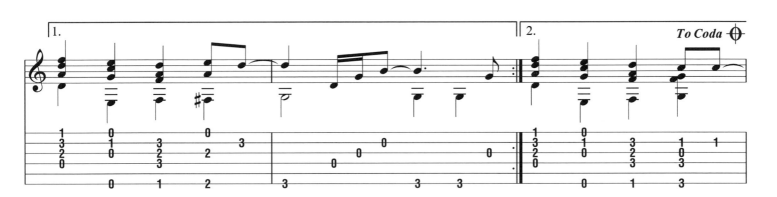

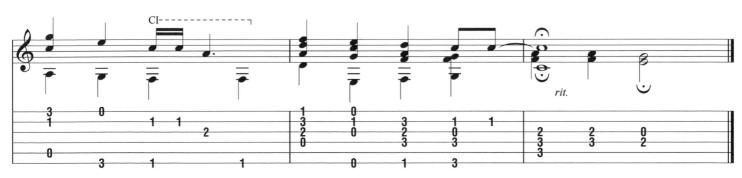

Can't Help Falling in Love

from the Paramount Picture BLUE HAWAII

Words and Music by
George David Weiss, Hugo Peretti
and Luigi Creatore

Moderately slow

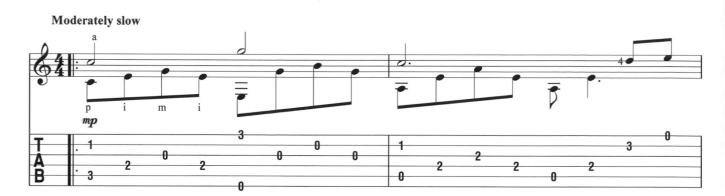

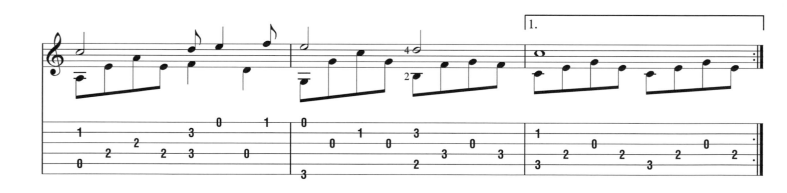

Chim Chim Cher-ee

from Walt Disney's MARY POPPINS

Words and Music by
Richard M. Sherman and Robert B. Sherman

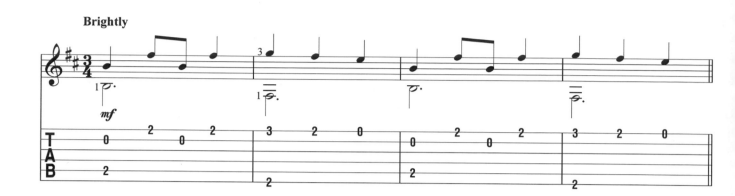

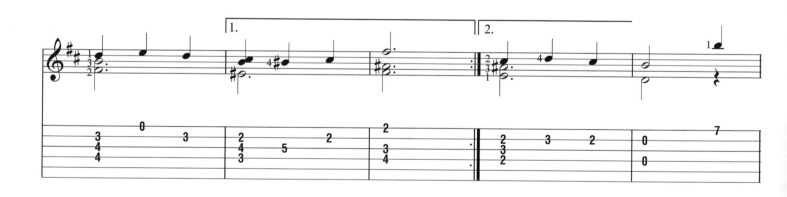

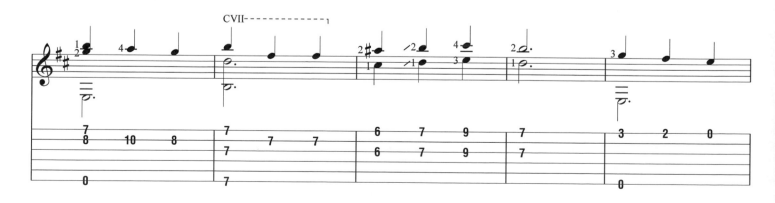

15

The First Cut Is the Deepest

Words and Music by Cat Stevens

Drop D tuning:
(low to high) D-A-D-G-B-E

Moderately

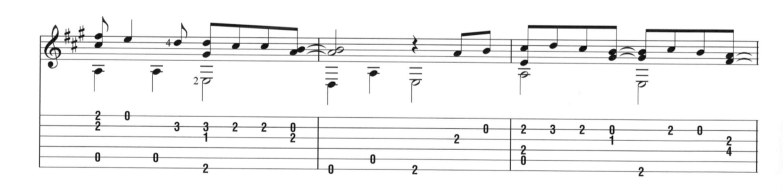

Hello

Words and Music by Lionel Richie

Moderately slow

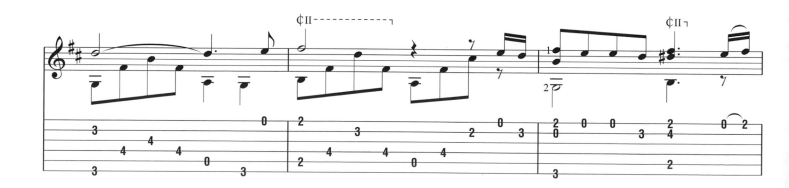

I Don't Know How to Love Him

from JESUS CHRIST SUPERSTAR

Words by Tim Rice
Music by Andrew Lloyd Webber

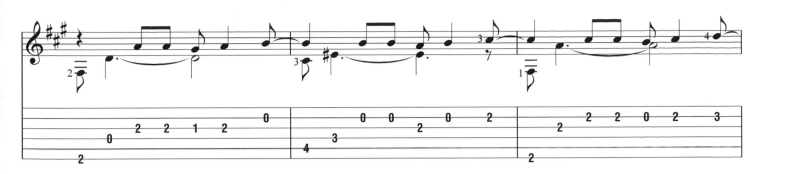

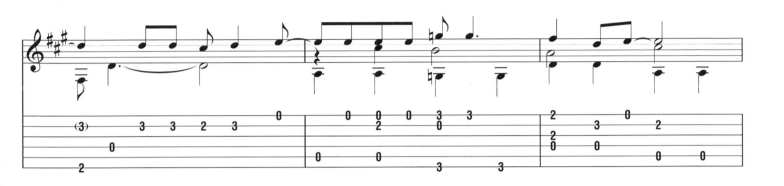

D.C. al Coda

Coda

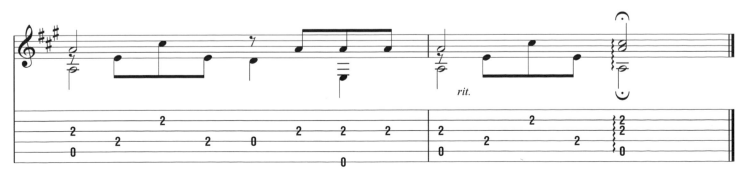

I Will Always Love You

Words and Music by Dolly Parton

Moderately slow

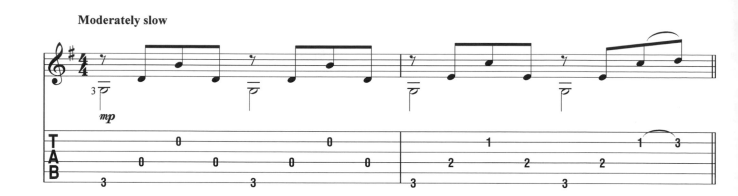

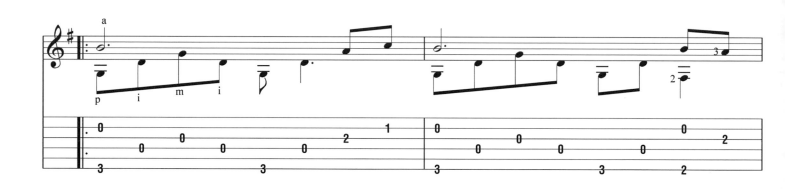

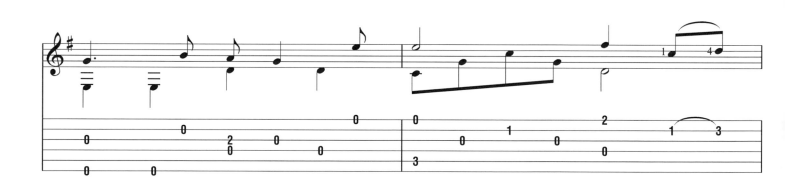

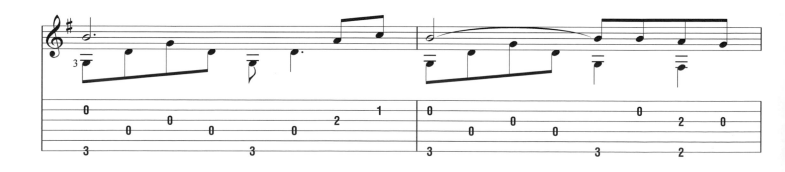

Killing Me Softly with His Song

Words by Norman Gimbel
Music by Charles Fox

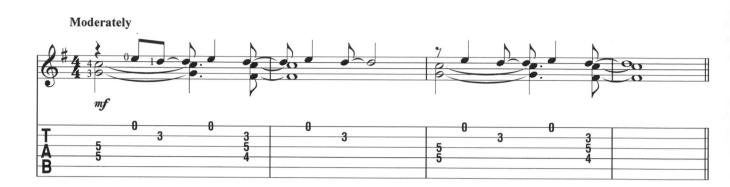

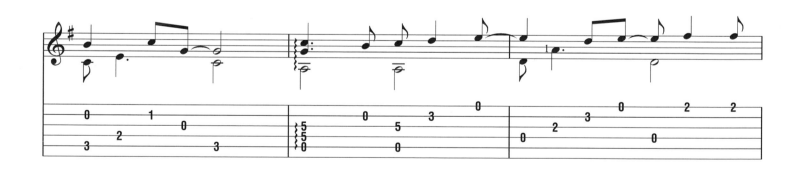

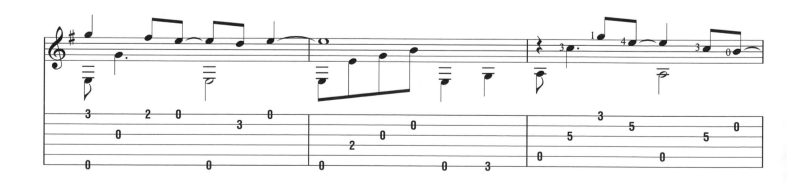

25

Moon River

from the Paramount Picture BREAKFAST AT TIFFANY'S

Words by Johnny Mercer
Music by Henry Mancini

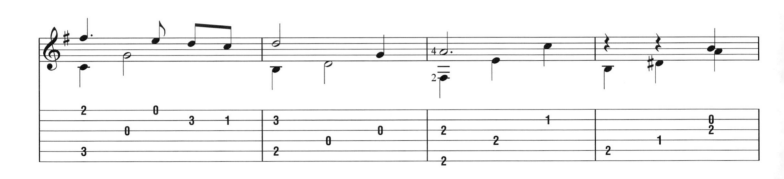

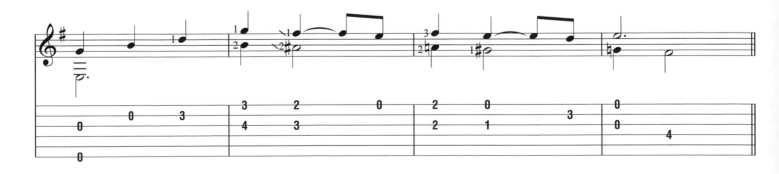

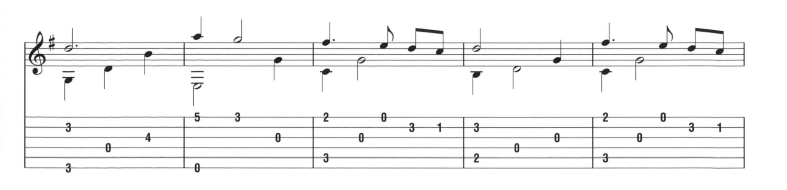

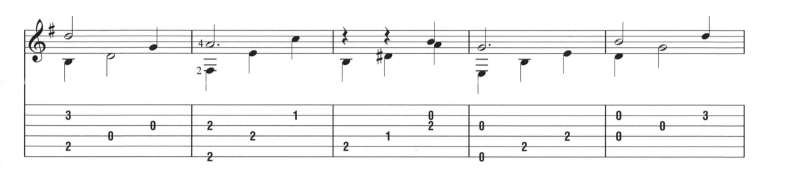

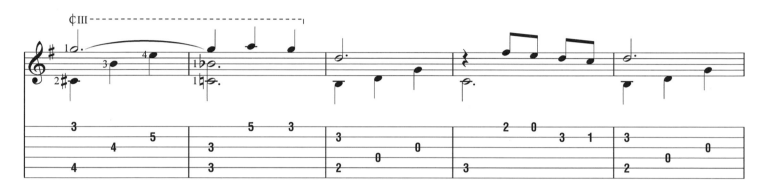

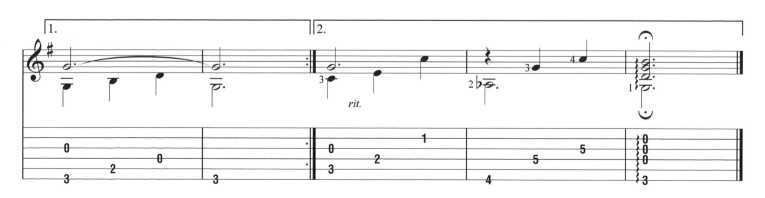

Morning Has Broken

Words by Eleanor Farjeon
Music by Cat Stevens

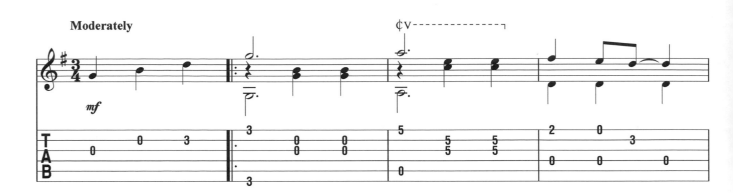

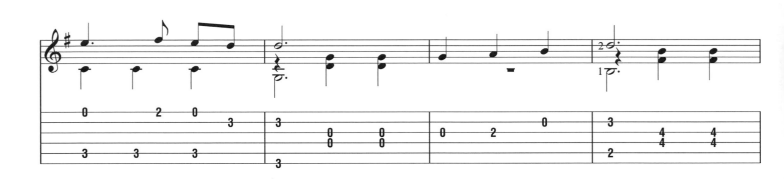

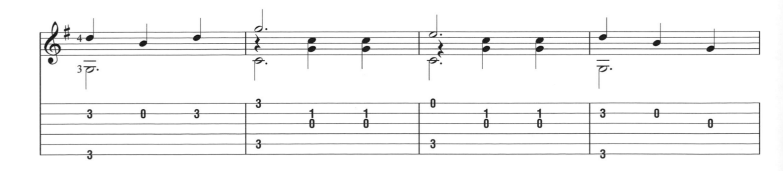

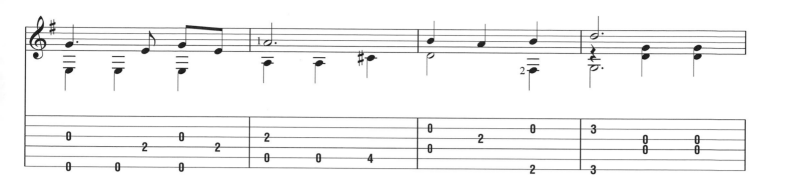

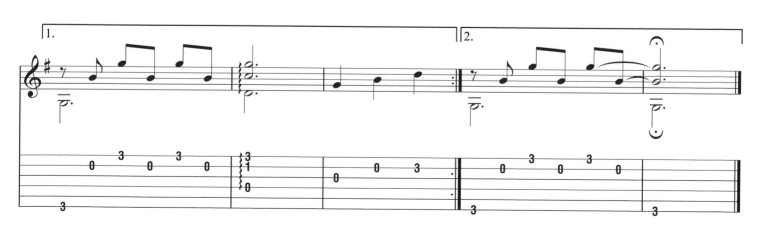

Suzanne

Words and Music by Leonard Cohen

Moderately

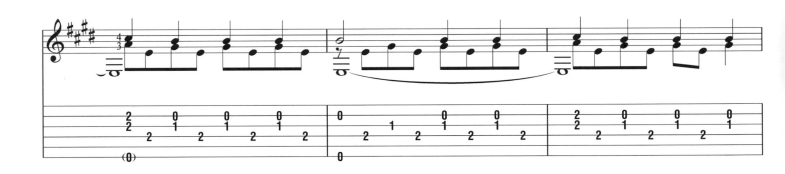

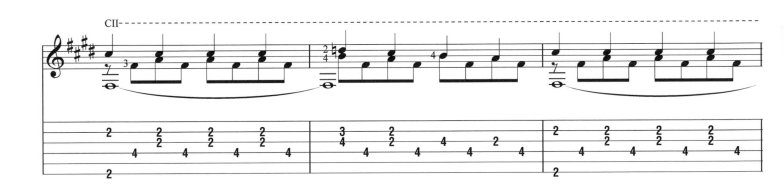

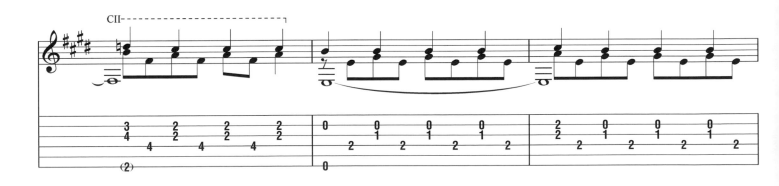

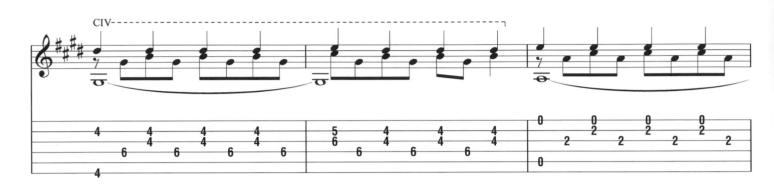

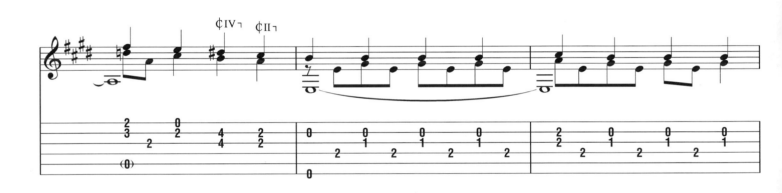

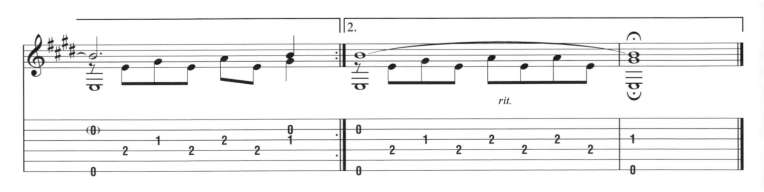

Up Where We Belong

from the Paramount Picture AN OFFICER AND A GENTLEMAN

Words by Will Jennings
Music by Buffy Sainte-Marie and Jack Nitzsche

Moderately slow

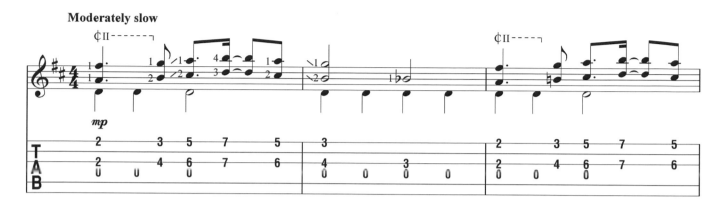

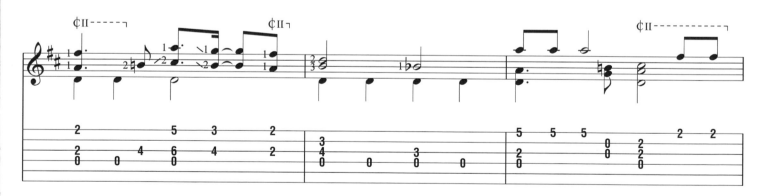

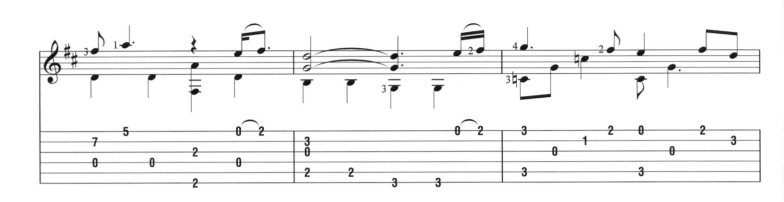

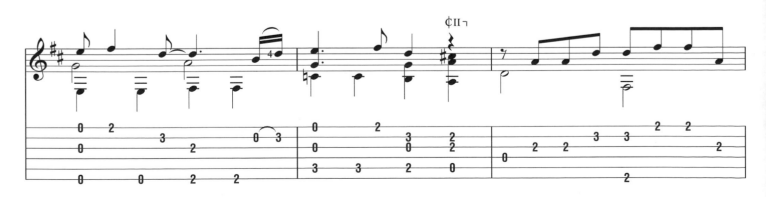

A Time for Us (Love Theme)

from the Paramount Picture ROMEO AND JULIET

Words by Larry Kusik and Eddie Snyder
Music by Nino Rota

Moderately

To Coda ⊕

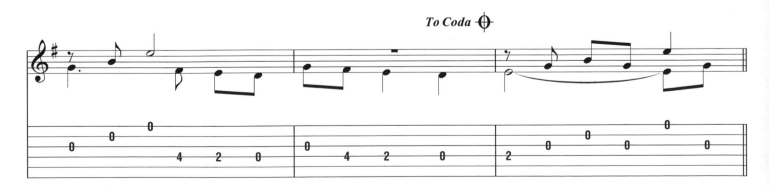

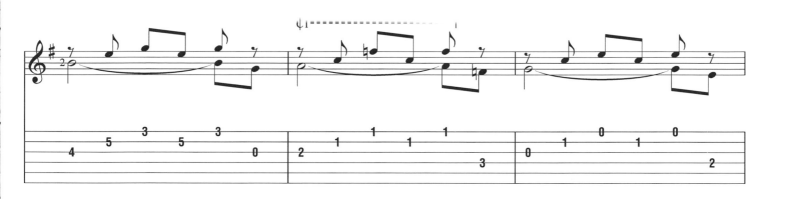

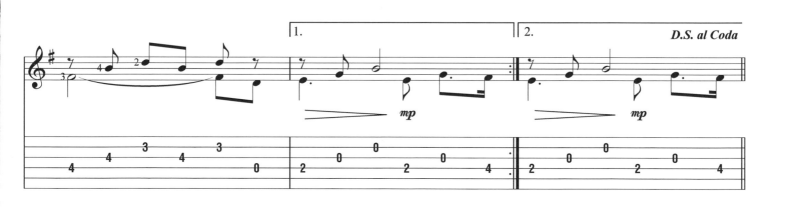

Unchained Melody

Lyric by Hy Zaret
Music by Alex North

Moderately

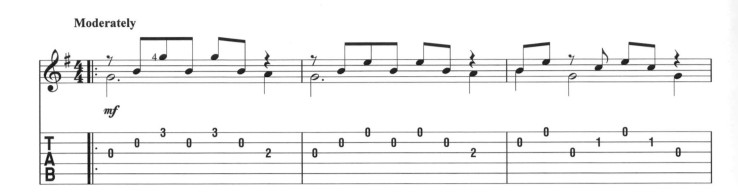

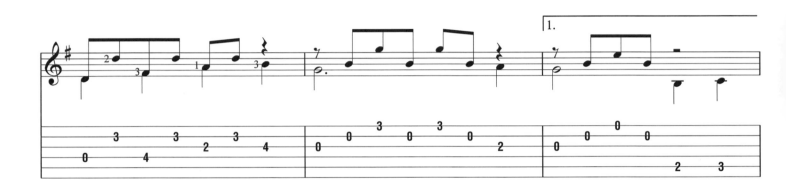

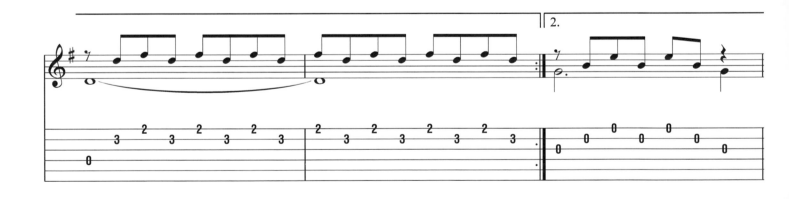

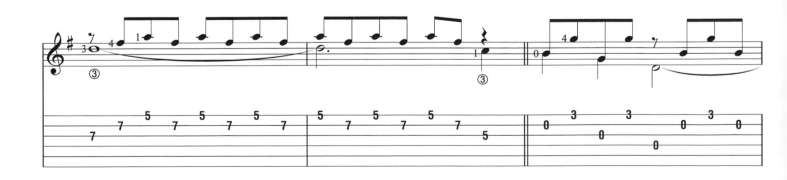

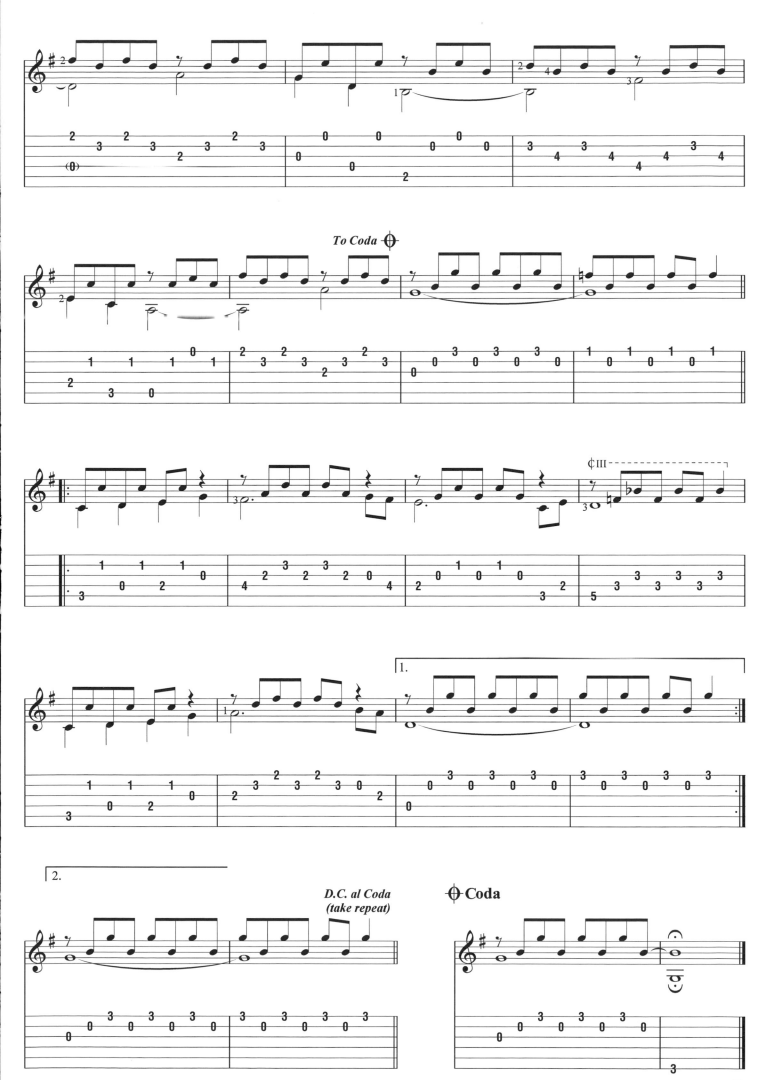

What a Wonderful World

Words and Music by
George David Weiss and Bob Thiele

Moderately slow, in 2

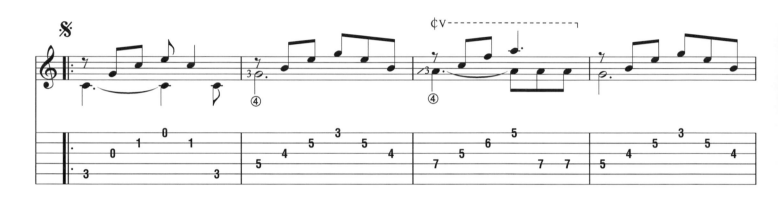

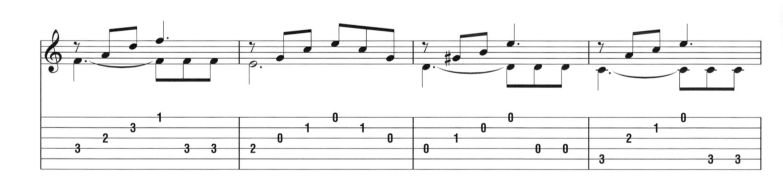

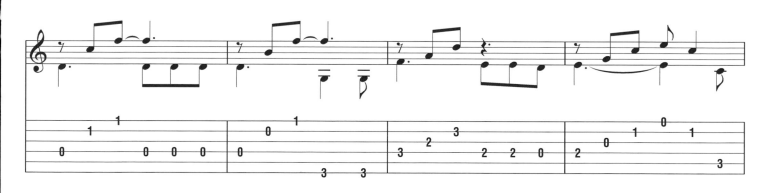

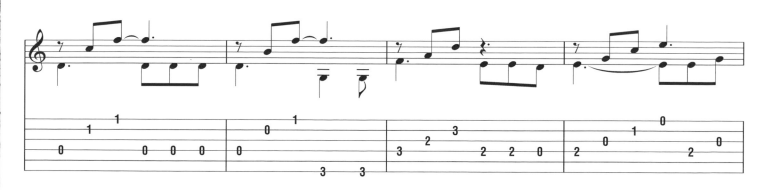

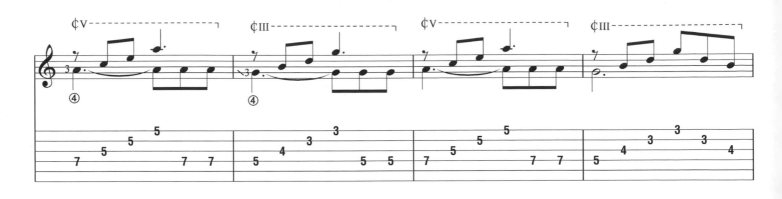

D.S. al Coda
(no repeat)

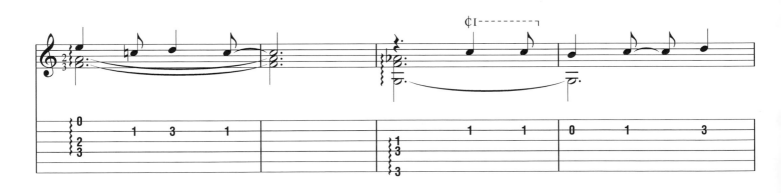

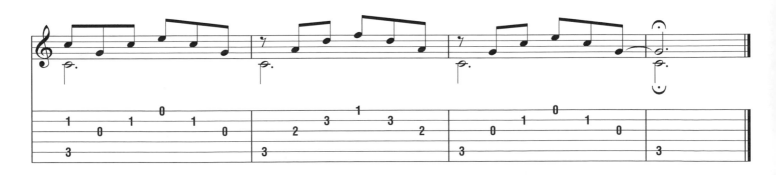

When She Loved Me

from Walt Disney Pictures' TOY STORY 2 - A Pixar Film

Music and Lyrics by Randy Newman

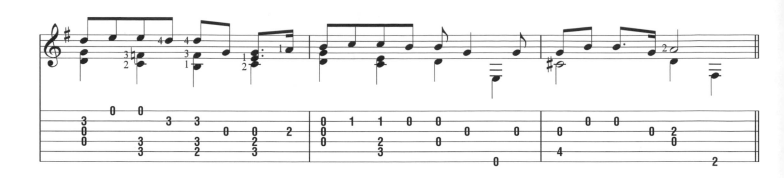

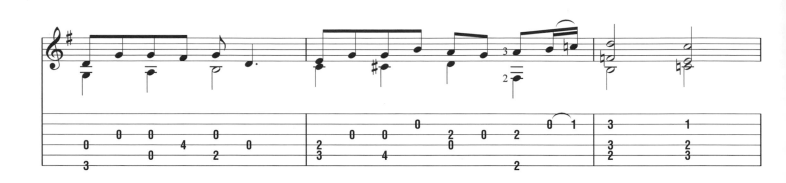

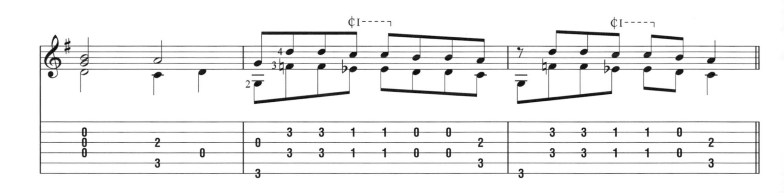

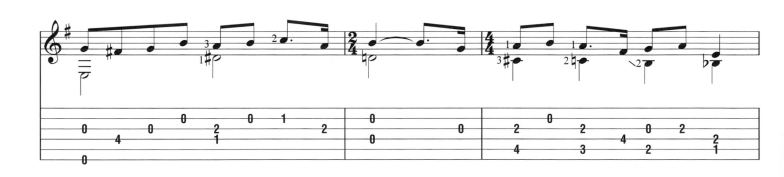

A Whole New World (Aladdin's Theme)

from Walt Disney's ALADDIN

Music by Alan Menken
Lyrics by Tim Rice

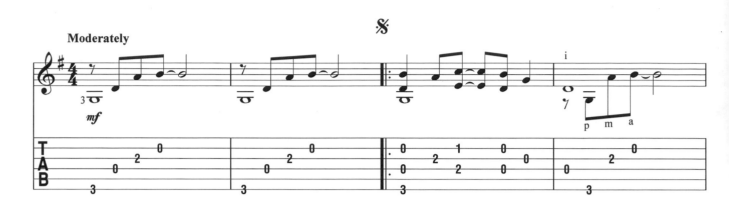

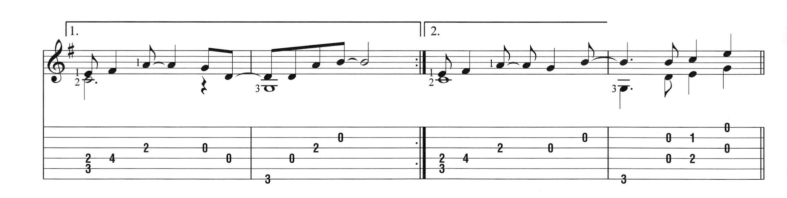

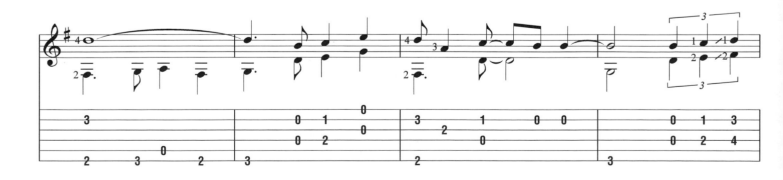

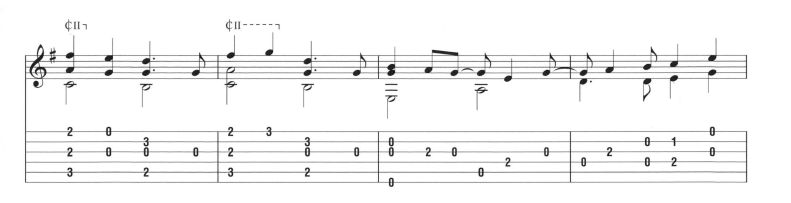

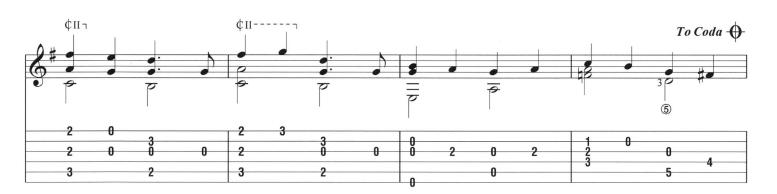

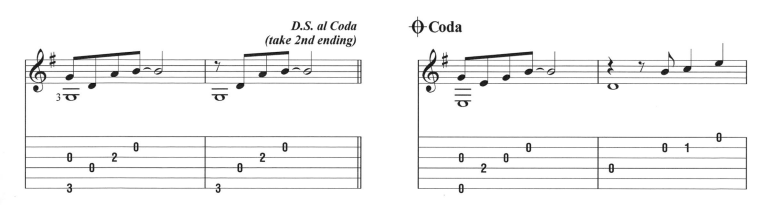

CLASSICAL GUITAR

INSTRUCTIONAL BOOKS & METHODS AVAILABLE FROM HAL LEONARD

CLASSICAL STUDIES FOR PICK-STYLE GUITAR
by William Leavitt
Berklee Press

This Berklee Workshop, featuring over 20 solos and duets by Bach, Carcassi, Paganini, Sor and other renowned composers, is designed to acquaint intermediate to advanced pick-style guitarists with some of the excellent classical music that is adaptable to pick-style guitar. With study and practice, this workshop will increase a player's knowledge and proficiency on this formidable instrument.
50449440..$12.99

ÉTUDES SIMPLES FOR GUITAR
by Leo Brouwer
Editions Max Eschig

This new, completely revised and updated edition includes critical commentary and performance notes. Each study is accompanied by an introduction that illustrates its principal musical features and technical objectives, complete with suggestions and preparatory exercises.
50565810 Book/CD Pack......................................$26.99

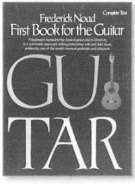

FIRST BOOK FOR THE GUITAR
by Frederick Noad
G. Schirmer, Inc.

A beginner's manual to the classical guitar. Uses a systematic approach using the interesting solo and duet music written by Noad, one of the world's foremost guitar educators. No musical knowledge is necessary. Student can progress by simple stages. Many of the exercises are designed for a teacher to play with the students. Will increase student's enthusiasm, therefore increasing the desire to take lessons.
50334370 Part 1 ....$12.99
50334520 Part 2 ....$17.99
50335160 Part 3 ....$16.99
50336760 Complete Edition..................................$32.99

HAL LEONARD CLASSICAL GUITAR METHOD
INCLUDES TAB
by Paul Henry

This comprehensive and easy-to-use beginner's guide uses the music of the master composers to teach you the basics of the classical style and technique. Includes pieces by Beethoven, Bach, Mozart, Schumann, Giuliani, Carcassi, Bathioli, Aguado, Tarrega, Purcell, and more. Includes all the basics plus info on PIMA technique, two- and three-part music, time signatures, key signatures, articulation, free stroke, rest stroke, composers, and much more.
00697376 Book/Online Audio (no tab) $16.99
00142652 Book/Online Audio (with tab) $17.99

A MODERN APPROACH TO CLASSICAL GUITAR
by Charles Duncan

This multi-volume method was developed to allow students to study the art of classical guitar within a new, more contemporary framework. For private, class or self-instruction.

00695114 Book 1 – Book Only...............................$8.99
00695113 Book 1 – Book/Online Audio.................$12.99
00699204 Book 1 – Repertoire Book Only.............$11.99
00699205 Book 1 – Repertoire Book/Online Audio .$16.99
00695116 Book 2 – Book Only...............................$7.99
00695115 Book 2 – Book/Online Audio.................$12.99
00699208 Book 2 – Repertoire.............................$12.99
00699202 Book 3 – Book Only...............................$9.99
00695117 Book 3 – Book/Online Audio.................$14.99
00695119 Composite Book/CD Pack....................$32.99

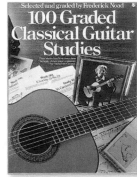

100 GRADED CLASSICAL GUITAR STUDIES
Selected and Graded by Frederick Noad

Frederick Noad has selected 100 studies from the works of three outstanding composers of the classical period: Sor, Giuliani, and Carcassi. All these studies are invaluable for developing both right hand and left hand skills. Students and teachers will find this book invaluable for making technical progress. In addition, they will build a repertoire of some of the most melodious music ever written for the guitar.
14023154..$29.99

CHRISTOPHER PARKENING GUITAR METHOD
THE ART & TECHNIQUE OF THE CLASSICAL GUITAR

Guitarists will learn basic classical technique by playing over 50 beautiful classical pieces, 26 exercises and 14 duets, and through numerous photos and illustrations. The method covers: rudiments of classical technique, note reading and music theory, selection and care of guitars, strategies for effective practicing, and much more!
00696023 Book 1/Online Audio $22.99
00695228 Book 1 (No Audio) $14.99
00696024 Book 2/Online Audio $22.99
00695229 Book 2 (No Audio) $14.99

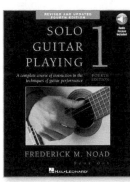

SOLO GUITAR PLAYING
by Frederick M. Noad

Solo Guitar Playing can teach even the person with no previous musical training how to progress from simple single-line melodies to mastery of the guitar as a solo instrument. Fully illustrated with diagrams, photographs, and over 200 musical exercises and repertoire selections, these books offer instruction in every phase of classical guitar playing.
14023147 Book 1/Online Audio $34.99
14023153 Book 1 (Book Only)..............................$24.99
14023151 Book 2 (Book Only)..............................$19.99

TWENTY STUDIES FOR THE GUITAR
ANDRÉS SEGOVIA EDITION
by Fernando Sor
Performed by Paul Henry

20 studies for the classical guitar written by Beethoven's contemporary, Fernando Sor, revised, edited and fingered by the great classical guitarist Andres Segovia. These essential repertoire pieces continue to be used by teachers and students to build solid classical technique. Features 50-minute demonstration audio.
00695012 Book/Online Audio $22.99
00006363 Book Only..$9.99

HAL•LEONARD®

Order these and more publications
from your favorite music retailer at
halleonard.com

Prices, contents and availability subject to change without notice.